VIEWPOINTS

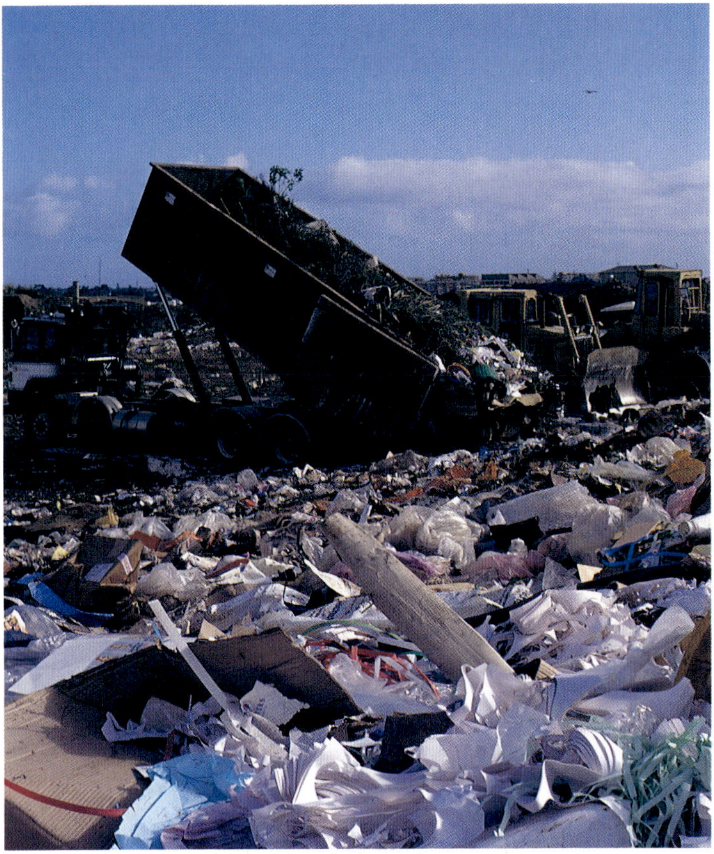

by Rodney Martin

CONTENTS

Introduction	3
What are the problems?	4
Household waste	4
Products and their effects	7
What are the solutions?	9
Recycling paper	12
Recycling household waste	13
Who is responsible?	15
Index	17
Glossary	17

INTRODUCTION

This book discusses the problem of waste disposal from different points of view.

Six people, who play different roles, were interviewed about their opinions on the following questions.

- What are the problems with waste disposal?
- How should these problems be solved?
- Who is responsible for solving these problems?

Interviewee	Role
Ron Patrick	*Plastics manufacturer*
Phillip Graham	*Government health inspector*
Dudley Williams	*Manager of a waste disposal company*
Lynette Thorstensen	*Greenpeace spokesperson*
Romeo Panazzolo	*Householders*
Maria Panazzolo	

WHAT ARE THE PROBLEMS?

People are creating more waste than ever before. In the USA, about one tonne of waste per person is created each year. This is the highest amount in the world.

"Our basic problem is we are a throw away society." (Dudley Williams)

Household waste

How much we throw away

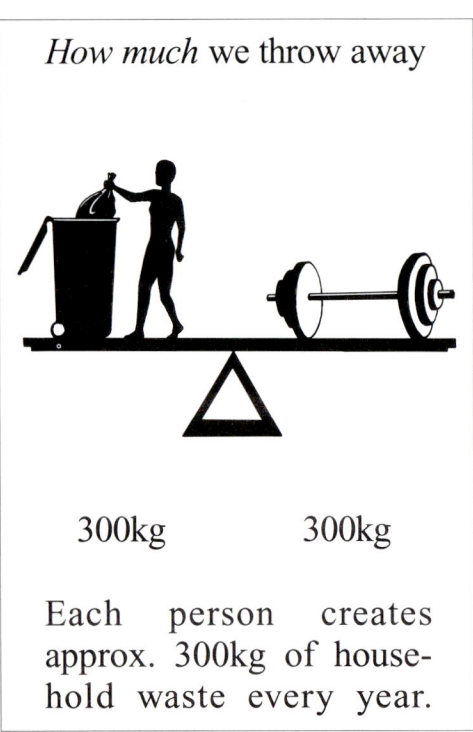

300kg   300kg

Each person creates approx. 300kg of household waste every year.

What we throw away

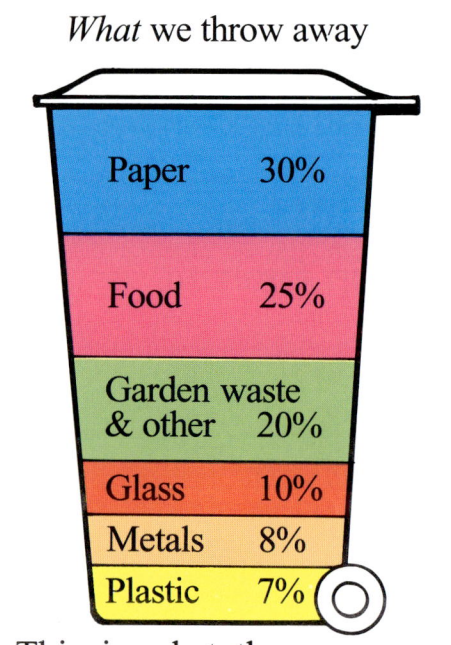

Paper	30%
Food	25%
Garden waste & other	20%
Glass	10%
Metals	8%
Plastic	7%

This is what the average household throws away in the waste bin.

The problems with waste include:
- the amount of waste created by our 'throw away society';
- space needed to dispose of waste;
- the expense of waste disposal;
- damage to the environment;
- toxic waste.

FACT!

In the North Sea toxic waste has caused skin diseases on fish.

Waste enters our environment as solids, liquids and gases. Many of these wastes are harmful to humans and other lifeforms.

FACT!

About 1 million sea birds are killed each year by plastic waste.

This bird died because it became caught in a plastic ring. As the bird grew the ring slowly cut into its neck and choked it.

Products and their effects

Batteries contain heavy metals (lead, mercury). These metals create toxic waste at landfill sites.

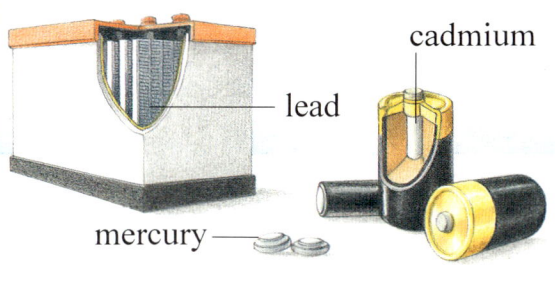

Power plants and vehicles pollute the air with toxic gases.

Many communities pipe sewage into coastal waters. This makes shellfish and other seafoods harmful to humans.

FACT!

Each person wastes about two trees' worth of paper each year.

The manufacture of foam cups creates CFCs that attack the ozone layer.

". . . we will run out of space. We can't treat the environment as if we are sweeping the dirt under the carpet."
(Lynette Thorstensen)

"The mixing of toxic waste with normal waste is a problem. We don't know what goes in the waste truck."
(Dudley Williams)

"It is expensive for the government to collect garbage. It's a long term problem . . . it's not going to go away."
(Phillip Graham)

WHAT ARE THE SOLUTIONS?

"We need safe products which don't produce poisons."
(Lynette Thorstensen)

IDEA!

Take a string bag to the supermarket.

One solution to the problems discussed in this book is to create less waste. For example, people can:
- buy non-toxic products and refuse to buy goods in unnecessary packaging;
- persuade politicians to protect the environment;
- recycle waste.

Industry is gradually finding ways to recycle products. Many new ideas are being researched.

FACT!

Old computers and other electronic equipment can be recycled to obtain gold.

The inner layer of this stormwater drain is made from recycled plastic bottles.

"Landfill sites produce gases. We can use these gases to generate electricity." (Dudley Williams)

FACT!

In the USA and Britain, people have died from gas explosions at old landfill sites.

This equipment collects methane gas from a landfill site. The gas is used as energy for homes.

Recycling paper

1. Cartons and paper are collected and pressed into blocks.

IDEA!

Make your own greeting cards from recycled paper.

2. These blocks are placed with water into a machine like a big food blender.

3. After 30 minutes the paper pulp is ready.

4. The pulp is then cleaned and placed on a paper-making machine.

Recycling household waste

IDEA!

Reduce toxic waste. Use rechargeable batteries.

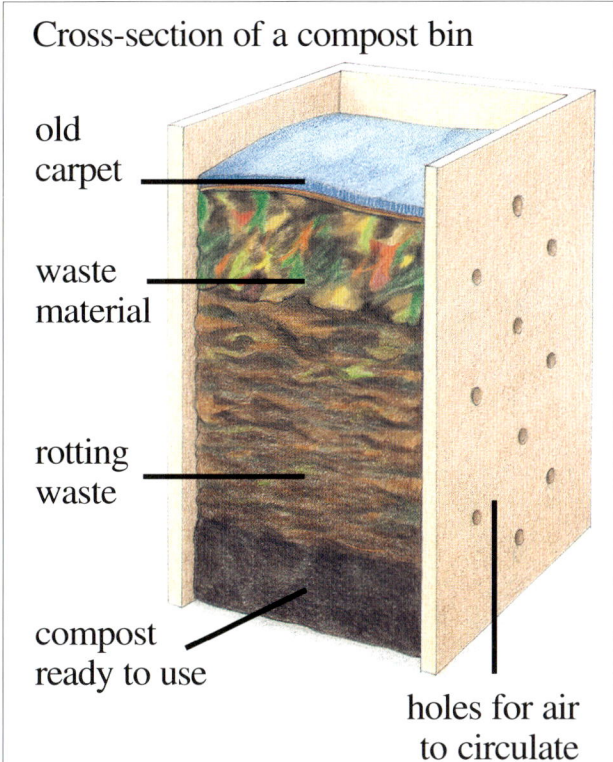

Cross-section of a compost bin
- old carpet
- waste material
- rotting waste
- compost ready to use
- holes for air to circulate

Kitchen and garden waste can be recycled in a compost bin. This makes excellent fertilizer for the garden.

"We don't waste much. Birds eat leftover bread and lettuce. Our dog eats leftover bones. We dig other leftover food into the garden." (Romeo Panazzolo)

13

"I remember the days when people used their own basket. Today the supermarket gives you a plastic bag, then they throw away their cardboard cartons." (Maria Panazzolo)

"We can use glass containers, not plastic, where possible. Glass is easily recycled."
(Lynette Thorstensen)

"Recycled plastic can be used for flower pots, fence posts, garden hoses . . . The plastics industry is coding different types of plastics with a number system. If they are collected and sorted, plastics can be recycled." (Ron Patrick)

WHO IS RESPONSIBLE?

People are beginning to realize that we are all responsible for solving problems with waste ... at home, at work, or wherever we might be.

"It has to be a shared responsibility ... between the people we elect for government, the people who make decisions in factories ... it has to be a responsibility for each of us."
(Lynette Thorstensen)

"Everybody is responsible."
(Maria Panazzolo)

"It's everybody's responsibility. It comes back to industry and the consumer to recycle wherever possible."
(Ron Patrick)

"The government should make laws to limit the use of plastic." (Romeo Panazzolo)

"The younger generation could be taught to be more responsible in the type of products they buy. Government and industry could look at new technology. The best we can hope for is for everyone to pull together as a team."
(Dudley Williams)

"Australian Aboriginal people lived for more than 40,000 years without having a waste problem. A kangaroo was used for food, then the carcass was used for many other things . . . the fur to keep warm, the bones and sinews for different implements. They didn't waste anything."
(Phillip Graham)